8/90

D0872282

FOREWORD

"Frontiers of America" dramatizes some of the explorations and discoveries of real pioneers in simple, uncluttered text. America's spirit of adventure is seen in these early people who faced dangers and hardship blazing trails, pioneering new water routes, becoming Western heroes as well as legends, and building log forts and houses as they settled in the wilderness.

Although today's explorers and adventurers face different frontiers, the drive and spirit of these early pioneers in America's past still serve as an inspiration.

ABOUT THE AUTHOR

During her years as a teacher and reading consultant in elementary schools, Mrs. McCall developed a strong interest in the people whose pioneering spirit built our nation. When she turned to writing as a full-time occupation, this interest was the basis for much of her work. She is the author of many books and articles for children and adults, and co-author of elementary school social studies textbooks.

Frontiers of America

HUNTERS
BLAZE THE TRAILS

By Edith McCall

Illustrations
By Carol Rogers

CHILDRENS PRESS, CHICAGO

Library of Congress Cataloging in
Publication Data
McCall, Edith S
   Hunters blaze the trails.
   1.   The West—Hist.   I.   Title.
PZ7,M1299.Hu   59-3666
ISBN 0-516-03332-8

REAL MEN and THEIR STORIES

DAVY CROCKETT, BEAR HUNTER

The days of Daniel Boone and Simon Kenton and the other hunters who led the way into Kentucky were over. The frontier was moving quickly to the west. But always it was the hunter or the trapper who was first in the wilderness, coming back with his furs and his stories of new and wonderful lands.

So it was that Davy Crockett, who would rather hunt than eat or sleep, kept moving farther west across the state of Tennessee. By 1826, he and his family were living in a log cabin not far from the Mississippi River. Davy had found a good place for hunting bears.

"How many did you get this time, Davy?" asked one of his neighbors when Davy came home from a week of bear hunting.

"Seventeen. Seventeen fine big bears, McDaniel," answered Davy.

"Sure wish I knew how you did it, Crockett," said McDaniel. "My wife and I could use some good bear meat. The grease and the fur would be mighty useful, too."

Crockett said, "I'll give you some of mine, McDaniel. Or, if you like, I'll take you hunting. You can get some for yourself."

McDaniel looked pleased. "That's mighty fine of you, Davy. I reckon my wife would be right proud if I could shoot a bear for her."

So it was that McDaniel, Davy Crockett and Davy's oldest son set out with Davy's eight hunting dogs, horses, guns and a good supply of ammunition.

"I'll take you to the *hurricane* to find you a bear," said Davy to McDaniel.

McDaniel said, "Just what do you mean by that? I thought a hurricane was a big wind."

Davy laughed. "It is, it is," he said. "And the place I mean is so full of fallen trees that you can see that a mighty big hurricane went through it. And that isn't all. We call it the *shakes* because it was so shaken up by the earthquakes of 1812 that it is full of cracks."

"Sounds like mighty rough country," said McDaniel. "Why do we want to go there?"

"Good places for bears to hide in the winter," said Davy. "The bears move out when the settlers move in, and that's about the only place left this side of the Mississippi that isn't taken up for farms. I sure hope we aren't too late to get you a bear or two."

"Why, just last week you killed seventeen!" said McDaniel.

"Hold on, friend!" said Davy. "We'll find some. But last week was before the big storm, and it wasn't nearly as cold as it is now. Likely the bears will be mostly all holed up in caves or hollow trees by now. But we'll get you one."

The pack of dogs had run on ahead, trying to pick up the trail of a bear. The two men and the boy could hear their yelps and barks.

"How do you know when they have found a bear?" asked McDaniel.

"I reckon you'll know, too" grinned Davy. "You'll hear old Tiger and Brutus and Carlo sing out in a special way. They'll open up and really holler. And that will be their way of sayin' to me, *Come on, Davy. We've got a bear for you. Just come and finish him off.*"

Davy's son laughed. "And don't ever try to stop Pa then. His dogs call — he goes. He and *Old Betsey* always answer the dogs' call."

"And who is *Betsey?* Another dog?" asked McDaniel.

Davy rubbed his hand along the barrel of his rifle.

9

"*Old Betsey* is my gun. Can't get along without her."

They rode on over fields and through the woods. When they came to a stream, dogs, horses and all walked or swam across. The day was almost over when they came to a ditch about six feet deep.

"Looks as if the earth just split open here," said McDaniel.

"It did," said Davy. "We're in the beginning of the *shakes* now. The *hurricane* is not far ahead."

Suddenly, the dogs' voices filled with excitement.

"A bear!" cried Davy. "Come on, McDaniel."

They hurried their horses along until they could see the dogs. Sure enough, they had a bear! The big animal stood on its hind legs, its back against a tree trunk. Dog after dog would leap at the bear's throat, only to be pushed back by a giant paw. They had been trained to keep the bear busy until their master could come near enough to shoot.

The men and the boy jumped down from their horses.

"I'll get him! I'll get him!" called McDaniel. He was taking aim with his rifle.

"Look out for my dogs!" cried Davy. "Hold it a

minute. Ready now? I'll call the dogs off and you fire the instant they turn."

Davy let out a sharp whistle, and the dogs jumped back. McDaniel's rifle cracked, and the bear came down.

"Good shot!" called Davy. He lowered his rifle. He had been ready to follow McDaniel's shot with one of *Old Betsey's* sure-fire bear killers. "Finish him off, McDaniel."

McDaniel went in closer and shot again at the wounded bear. This time, the animal lay still.

Davy took his knife from his belt. With the quickness of long practice, he made cuts to skin the bear. He set the hide fur-side down and loaded the best chunks of fat and meat onto it. When this was done, the hide was wrapped around the meat, and the bundle packed onto one of the horses which had been brought along to carry home the bears.

McDaniel was pleased with himself.

"Do you think we will get another one today?" he asked.

"Might be, but it is getting late," said Davy.

The dogs had rushed off into the woods again, but they found no more bears that day. The three hunters rode off as darkness came, to find the cabin of an old friend. Davy Crockett had friends all over the state of Tennessee, and he was always a welcomed visitor.

The next morning they were on their way early, heading back toward Davy's *hurricane*. They had gone about five miles without hearing any signal from the dogs. McDaniel and the boy were riding ahead when Davy saw something that made him stop.

As he got off his horse he called to the others, "Come back here, boys! There's a bear up in this old tree!"

They tied the horses a little way off and walked back to the tree.

"How do you know?" asked McDaniel.

"See those scratch marks on the bark?" asked Davy.

McDaniel nodded. "Yes, I see them. But how do you know the bear didn't come down again?"

"No, he's in that hole up there." Davy pointed to a hole about twenty feet up the rotted tree trunk. "The marks are short—the kind a bear makes when he climbs a tree. If he had come down again, there would be long scratches in the bark, because he slips coming down. That old fellow is still in there, and he's a big one!"

"How are we going to get him out where we can shoot him?" asked McDaniel.

Davy had been thinking about the same thing. He pointed to a smaller tree about twenty feet from the one which held the bear.

"We'll cut that tree and let it fall against the big one. The boy here will climb up and look right in on old Mr. Bear. He can shoot him while he is still in his hole, and then we'll chop down the tree."

Davy took his tomahawk from his belt and walked over to the smaller tree and began to chop at it. It was slow work without a real ax, but each of the three took turns at chopping. They had worked at it only a short time when they heard the dogs "open up" somewhere ahead in the woods.

"Son, you stay here and work at this tree while McDaniel and I go after that one!" cried Davy. He had picked up his rifle and was already on the way. Just ahead, the great number of fallen trees marked the edge of the hurricane's path. There was no use trying to ride to the place where the dogs had treed their bear, so the men went on foot.

Davy reached the place ahead of McDaniel.

"They have a good fat one!" he called back.

As McDaniel came nearer, he could see the dogs leaping up trying to reach a dark form in the tree. But the bear had climbed above their reach, and was resting in the fork of a big limb. The dogs were trying to climb the tree, too. But they only fell back to the ground. They yelped and barked loud enough to be heard for miles.

Davy was aiming *Old Betsey.*

"Stay back, McDaniel," he said. "Sometimes they come down from the tree when they see a man with a gun. That is hard on the dogs. I'll shoot him from here, before he sees us."

But McDaniel, remembering his lucky shot of the day before, was taking aim, too.

"Let me have him, Crockett," he said. "I'd like to be able to tell my wife I killed him. If I miss, you pick him off."

Davy nodded.

McDaniel's rifle blazed. His aim was good, and the bear fell to the ground like a great log. The dogs backed off to get out of the way, and then rushed in on the great bear to finish him off if need be.

"You'll make a bear hunter yet, McDaniel," said Crockett. He stepped into the bunch of excited dogs. "We don't need you fellows now. Let him be."

The well-trained dogs turned away from the dead bear and began to sniff about for a new trail to follow.

15

In the sudden quiet, Davy's ears picked up a far-off sound. He looked down at his dogs and began counting them.

"One, two, three, four, five, six, seven—I thought that was Old Carlo I heard. He left the pack and has gone off and treed a bear all by himself." Davy was putting his knife into his belt and picking up his rifle. "I'll be back, McDaniel. You skin this one. He's yours, anyway."

Davy and his dogs were on their way to the third bear. Before McDaniel had finished butchering the second one, Davy was back, dragging bear number three in its skin. He helped McDaniel finish his work, and they took the two bundles of meat back to where the horses and Davy's son were waiting.

"Is he still up there, son?" Davy called.

The boy was swinging his tomahawk at the tree in which the bear was hiding. "He sure is, Pa. But I didn't do too well with chopping down the small tree. It fell too far to the side and missed this one. Guess we'll have to cut this one down to get that bear."

His tomahawk cut through into nothingness with the next stroke.

"This tree is rotten all the way through," he called.

McDaniel went to help the boy. "We'll have it down in a hurry," he said. "Get those dogs away, Crockett! This tree is going to come down fast!"

Davy called his dogs and hurried away with them. When he was about one hundred yards from the tree, he turned to look back. What he saw made the back of his neck prickle with sudden fear.

"Son! Look out, son! Get back! Get back, both of you!"

The two who had been chopping looked up. There was the bear, angry at having his sleep disturbed. He was climbing from the hole, snarling at the men below. McDaniel ran to get his gun, which was leaning against a tree with the other rifles.

"He's going to jump at you, son! Get back!" yelled Davy. He, too, was running toward the rifles.

Young Crockett jumped back. The bear came to the earth with a mighty leap. Before he could get to his feet, the pack of dogs was upon him.

The snarls of the bear were terrible to hear. He stood up after rolling about and struggling with the dogs. He had his back to the tree and struck out at the dogs as they leaped for his throat. His claws raked into the sides of the two who bit into his flesh. The cries of

the dogs and the snarling of the bear filled the air.

Then several of the dogs jumped at him at the same time, and the bear fell to the ground.

"I'll shoot him!" yelled McDaniel.

But Davy cried, "No! You'll get one of my dogs!"

Dogs and bears had rolled and tumbled farther and farther from the old tree. Davy made sure his rifle was loaded and ran after them. The boy watched in fear as his father rushed right into the middle of the snapping pack of animals.

"Pa! He'll get you!" he yelled.

But Davy Crockett knew what he was going to do, and did not give the bear time to attack him. He rushed in and pushed the end of his gun against the bear's chest.

The bullet went right into the bear's heart. The fight went out of him, and the dogs leaped upon him in joy.

McDaniel had been standing with his mouth open. Now he came to life again. He walked up to Crockett and held out his hand.

"Davy," he said, "I was beginning to think I could get any bear that you could get. But I wouldn't have done what you did for any bear or dog alive."

Davy's son looked up from the work of skinning the bear.

"My Pa is the greatest bear hunter in all of Tennessee," he said.

McDaniel smiled at Crockett. "Your boy knows what he is talking about," he said. "The greatest bear hunter in all of Tennessee and the rest of the country, too."

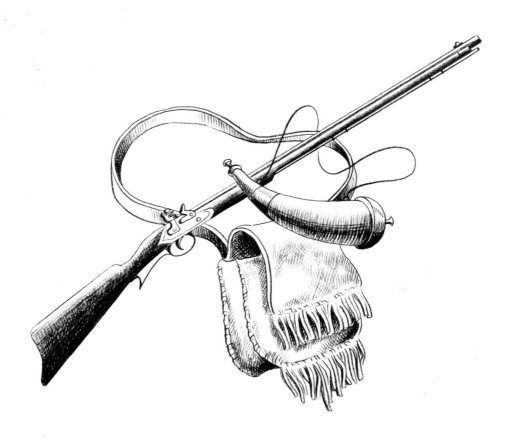

DAVY, THE BEAR AND THE PIT

Davy Crockett, his son and his neighbor had three bears for their day's work.

"Not bad," said Davy. "I often have chased all day after just one bear."

They set up camp in the woods that night. The bear meat would not spoil in the cold weather of January, but they had to put it where wolves could not reach it. They set four poles into the ground and made a platform with tree limbs. There they put their meat.

The next morning, McDaniel and Davy Crockett set out again, leaving Davy's son to take care of the camp. The two men rode their horses until they came to the beginning of the *hurricane.*

"We'll have to walk from here on," said Davy.

They tied their horses, and began to pick their way over the fallen trees. The dogs were far ahead. They could hear them baying.

"The dogs are coming back this way," said Davy. And sure enough, in a few minutes, five of his dogs came running towards the men.

"They look plum tuckered out," said Davy as he patted the head of first one and then another.

Mr. McDaniel looked "plum tuckered out", too. He was ready to go home.

"Davy, if the dogs can't pick up a bear's trail, is there any use in going on?" he asked.

Davy was not yet ready to give up. "Tell you what, McDaniel. We'll go on just a mite farther. If we don't find a bear holed up here in the *hurricane,* we'll go back."

They picked their way on a little farther. McDaniel was finding the brush and piles of dead wood very tiring to climb through and over. He was about to say he was going back when suddenly the dogs sniffed the air and leaped forward. Over the fallen trees they went, yelping loudly.

"Look there, McDaniel! There's your bear, not forty yards away!" called Crockett. "And I see the tracks of another. A regular screamer! Sounds like the rest of my hounds might have him treed. Good luck! See you later!"

Davy started off in the direction the tracks led. He didn't need to follow the tracks closely, for his dogs' yelps told him the way. But he had to go slowly, for he

came to a patch of briers and fallen trees and branches so thick that he had to get down on his knees and crawl through them.

"Coming, lads!" he called to his dogs as he at last came out the other side of the briers. He could see the dogs about one hundred feet ahead. They were leaping around the base of an old stump about twenty-feet high. On top, the bear was perched. It was an easy shot to bring him down.

"Well, dang the luck!" said Davy. "I've gone and lost my knife!" He was ready to skin the great beast, and looked all about for the knife that should have been in his belt. Just then he wheeled and reached for his rifle. Something was coming through the brier patch.

He had the gun reloaded when he heard his friend's voice.

"Are you looking for this, Davy?" There was Mc-Daniel holding up the knife.

"I followed your trail through the *hurricane* after I got my bear. I found this in the thickest part."

"Thank you, McDaniel," said Davy. "I'd almost as soon lose my hand as that knife. We'll make short work of this fellow now."

An hour later, the two men were very tired. They

had brought the horses as close as they could to the two butchered bears, but they had to make several trips through the fallen trees, carrying the furs and meat. It was almost sunset as they worked their way slowly back to their camp.

"Hello!" called Davy when he thought his son might hear.

"Hello!" came the answer.

"Not far," said Davy, "and I am not sorry. I am mighty tired."

McDaniel was about to answer when Davy held up his hand. The tiredness seemed to leave him as he listened.

"Hear that?" he said. "My dogs have another one! Here — take my horse to camp!" And he ran back towards the *hurricane.*

"Well, I'll be —" said McDaniel. "He's more of a bear hunter than I am, that I know!"

Davy himself began to wonder if it was worth it as he stumbled over fallen logs and into cracks left by the earthquakes. The sun set, and the woods darkened quickly.

"Sure would like to go back to camp," he thought,

25

"but I can't let those hounds down. They know I'll come."

He stumbled over the stump of a fallen tree.

"Too dark to see," he muttered. "I'll be lucky if I don't break my gun in one of these earthquake holes."

He had gone about three miles when he came to a creek. His body was so wet with sweat that he hardly felt the cold water as he waded through it. He fought his way through the thick growth along the creek, and then stopped to listen for his dogs.

"They've got him," he said aloud. "They've stopped running, and aren't too far from here."

He tried to move on straight toward the sounds, but the hillside was too steep. He circled around until he found a place where he could get up the hill. When he reached the top, his ears told him he had gone beyond the dogs. He turned again in the right direction.

"Ha! There you are!" he panted, as at last he came near the dogs. He stood in the darkness, trying to see where the bear was. At last his eyes made out the shape of the bear in the fork of a large tree. The dogs were leaping around the tree's trunk.

"Wish there was a moon tonight," he thought. "I'll have to make a fire to see by."

He pushed around with his toes at the ground, looking for some dry brush. But he found none. He did learn that the tree stood in a spot almost surrounded by large earthquake cracks. "Not too good," he said aloud.

He lifted his rifle and fired at the dark lump. He would have to reload fast. If he wounded the bear and it fell to the ground, he would need his gun quickly.

But the bear only moved higher into the tree.

"Aha!" said Davy. "Now I can see you better, my boy. We'll let *Old Betsey* have another try at you."

He fired, but the bear did not move. "How could I have missed him?" Davy muttered.

Then suddenly, the bear was down on the ground among the dogs. Davy worked to reload. The dogs and the snarling bear seemed to be everywhere.

"If only I could see!" he thought. The bear bumped against him, but it was only trying to fight off a dog. Davy dropped his rifle and reached for his long knife. He pulled it from its leather cover and held it ready if the bear should come near him again.

All he could see was the fast moving body of the one white dog he had. All the rest were dark colored, and their bodies and that of the bear could not be seen. Davy stood in the middle of a pool of sound and action, and he could do nothing. It was like a nightmare.

Then came the thud of a heavy falling body.

"He fell into one of the cracks!" thought Davy. He heard his dogs leap down after the huge bear. Following the sounds, Davy crawled to the edge of the pit.

"Not hard to tell which is the biting end," he thought. "Those poor dogs tell me that. It sounds to be about four feet deep. I'll push my rifle against him and fire."

As carefully as he could, Davy reached down into the pit, trying to judge about where the bear's heart would be. As soon as the muzzle of the gun touched the side of the beast, he fired. In a second, he leaped quickly back.

"That was close!" he muttered. The bear, only wounded, had jumped from the ditch. Once more, dogs and bear were rolling and tumbling about him.

Thud! The heavy body of the bear hit the bottom of a pit again. Davy reached for his gun, which he had dropped as he jumped back from the wounded bear.

"Where is it?" he said aloud. He felt around the ground, but he could not find the gun. His hand came onto something round and long, but it was not *Old Betsey*. It was a pole.

"I'll try punching him a while with this," he said. "My poor old dogs are getting right tired. I'll help wear out that old bear."

He leaned over the pit and poked and punched at the great animal. He felt the bear's teeth bite into the pole, and worked to push the beast backward. The dogs, free for a moment, leaped out of the pit and then down at the bear's throat. Davy felt the pole free again. He poked again and again, but the bear did not seem to be wearing out.

"That won't do it," said Davy. "I'll have to get down in there and finish him off."

The dogs seemed to know that their master was about to do something dangerous and that he needed their help. As Davy jumped down into the pit behind the bear, they all worked to keep the bear busy.

"Poor fellow!" thought Davy as he heard the cries of pain that came from one of his dogs. He pulled out his knife and held it ready.

"I'll have to do this fast, before he turns on me," thought Davy. His hand touched the bear's hip. He reached forward and placed his left hand on the bear's shoulder. Then down came his right arm and the knife plunged into the bear's body.

Without waiting to pull the knife, Davy climbed from the pit. He knew from the changed sound of the dogs' barking that the fight had gone out of the bear. The battle was won!

The night was long and cold. All of Davy's clothes were wet. As his tired body rested at last, the wetness made the cold more biting.

"Leather pants may be fine for keeping off the scratches," he said aloud. "But they are awful at a time like this. I'll have to keep moving, or I'll freeze to death."

His dogs were resting now, their work finished. Davy worked on, butchering the bear in the pit and lifting the chunks of meat up to the ground. His arms and legs pained him with every move. At last the butchering was finished, and he sat down to rest again.

But all too quickly the bite of the coldness of night in January cut into him.

"If I sleep, I'll surely die. After all this work, I can't just let this bear go to waste that way," he said aloud.

He crawled about, picking up bits of twigs and brush. After some time, he had a fire started. But almost everything about him was wet, and he could not keep the fire burning. Very little heat came from it. Davy jumped up and down to keep warm, even though he hurt all over. But that was not enough to keep out the chill.

He walked to a tree with a trunk about two-feet thick. There was not a limb on it for thirty feet up. He made himself climb the tree to the first limb. There he grasped his arms about the trunk, and let himself slide down. The rubbing of his body on the rough tree trunk made him feel almost warm.

All through the rest of the night, Davy made himself climb that tree, rest a moment, and then slide down. When daylight came at last, he started back over his trail towards the camp.

Before the day was over, Davy, his son and Mr. McDaniel were back at the pit, ready to take the bear back to camp.

McDaniel looked down into the pit where there were many signs of the fight that had taken place.

"Davy Crockett," he said, "I wouldn't have gone into that pit with a bear for all the meat in the world! You are not the greatest bear hunter of Tennessee and the United States. You are the greatest bear hunter in all the world!"

BEAVER TRAPPERS IN THE ROCKIES

In those same years that Kentucky and Tennessee were becoming too crowded for the hunters, news came of wonderful hunting grounds west of the Mississippi River. Before long, hundreds of Americans had set out to join hunting and trapping parties. They spread out all over the great west to the Rocky Mountains. The stories they told and the maps they made helped the people to learn about their country.

Beaver! The streams of the west held hundreds of the little animals whose fur brought a good price.

A chance to earn money, and to have a great adventure was ahead for those who went west. Many young men from the states in the east set out to join parties of trappers going into the wild land where no white men had made a home.

One of these young men was Zenas Leonard. He left his home in Pennsylvania and went to St. Louis, Missouri. There he got a job with a party of trappers under a man named Gant. Captain Gant led them to the Rocky Mountains. There the trappers divided into smaller parties and set out to trap beaver.

One day, a year after he had left St. Louis, young Zenas was "running his trap line." He walked into the water of the clear mountain stream in which he had set his traps. Not far ahead was one of the traps he had set the day before.

He could see a dark shape lying on the creek bottom not far from the edge of the stream.

"I caught another one," he said to himself. "And a good thing it is — I think we have just about cleaned out this stream of beaver, for the catch hasn't been good all week."

He had been trapping long enough to know that if he walked on land to his traps, the beaver would not go near them. The little animals knew that the smell of man meant traps near by. So Zenas always walked in the water when caring for his traps. He stooped and picked up the drowned beaver. The steel trap held tightly to its right front leg.

He took off the trap and held up the beaver. "A good one! It must weigh fifty pounds," he thought. The beaver was about thirty-six inches long.

Zenas put the beaver down again so that he could reset his trap. A six-foot length of heavy chain was at-

tached to the trap. At its other end, the chain was held by a heavy stick which Zenas had driven into the creek bed. The stick had been pulled almost free.

"He put up a good fight," Zenas said. He pounded the stick into the creek bed and piled some rocks about it. He put the trap in a place he had dug out near the bank. Tied to the trap with a piece of hair pulled from a horse's tail was a little stick about four inches long.

Zenas held this stick in his hand as he reached into his hunting shirt for a small horn bottle. From the bottle he poured a little thick yellow liquid into a hollowed-out place at one end of the stick.

"I never will learn to like the smell of this stuff," Zenas said. "But the beavers like it and that is what counts."

He pushed the other end of the stick into a crack in the bank of the creek just above the trap, so that it was about four inches above the water. If Zenas' luck held, another beaver would come swimming toward the stick after he had gone. The yellow liquid, castoreum, was taken from a beaver's body, and its smell seemed to draw the beavers to the trap. A beaver would swim near the stick, and as he reached for it one of his front paws would touch the trap. Snap! The trap would close. The beaver would try to get away, but the heavy trap would pull him down and he would drown.

Zenas knew that once his trap had sprung, other beaver would not be drawn by the smell of the castorum. That was why he tied it to the trap with a piece of horsehair — it would be pulled underwater, too. Instead of coming to that trap, other beavers would be drawn to one of the seven other traps Zenas had placed along the stream.

The last thing to do was to open the jaws of the trap. With that done, Zenas picked up the beaver and walked back through the stream to the place where he had left two more dead beavers. He had checked all his traps, and only three had been sprung. The spring trapping season was about over.

He set about skinning the three animals. He had a sharp knife for this job. Carefully, he cut the skin around the tail, inside the four legs, and down the center of the underside. He pulled the skin back, working it loose with his knife.

When the three furs where ready to be taken back to camp, Zenas looked back at the meat he was leaving. "When I think of how hungry we trappers were last winter, it seems a shame to waste it. But beaver meat does not taste good, and we have buffalo meat in camp. I'll take only the tails."

Beaver tail meat was good. Zenas thought of how very good it would have tasted when he and several other trappers had been caught in a snowstorm on a mountain that last winter. They had more than their share of trouble that winter, and almost all of it because they did not know much about life in the Rocky Mountains, or trapping either.

First, they had lost their horses because they had nothing to feed them. They heard that horses could get through a mountain winter if they had the bark of cottonwood trees to eat. So, when they made their winter camp, the trappers set about cutting a good supply of bark.

What they didn't know was that there is just one kind of cottonwood bark the horses will eat — the sweet kind.

They had cut a kind which the horses wouldn't touch. With no hay to eat, and no bark to take its place, the horses died one by one. Trappers needed horses to carry their supplies and their furs from one place to another.

"We'll go to Santa Fe and get some more horses," said the leader of their small group, whose name was Stephens. But he was not a very good mountaineer himself, and did not plan well for the eight-hundred-mile walk to the Mexican trading city. The men had been caught in heavy snows on the mountains. They could neither go on nor get back to camp. That was when they had almost died from hunger.

They chewed the hides of the beaver furs they had taken along to trade for horses. That was all they had to keep themselves alive, until the day a deer had come near. After that they had some strength and the snow melted enough so that they could get back to their camp in a river valley.

They were still in trouble, for they did not have very many furs to trade. Some had been stolen, and some lost.

Still without horses, they had gone to the place where they were supposed to meet Captain Gant. But there was no sign of him.

Zenas and two other trappers had gone up to the little stream where Zenas had just taken three beaver,

thinking they might get a few more furs while they waited for Captain Gant. It was a branch of the Laramie River in what later became the state of Wyoming.

When Zenas reached the camp, he found the other two trappers already there. They had started some buffalo meat cooking for supper over an open fire near the river bank.

"How was your catch, Zenas?" asked one of the men, whose name was Smith.

"Only three," said Zenas. He set about cutting willow branches on which to stretch the furs. "How about you?"

Smith said, "Fully and I trapped only five between us. I think the stream is about trapped out for this season." The five furs were off to one side on the ground, held open by the willow hoops. Smith and Fully were scraping clean the underside of some furs which had been stretched earlier.

Zenas worked in the shade of a rocky bluff which reached almost to the bank of the stream where they were camping. When his three furs were stretched out on their willow hoops, he picked up a fur from another pile and began rubbing it to take out some of the stiffness. That pile was ready for smoking — the last step before the furs were tied into bundles for taking to the traders.

Near by, the buffalo roast spit and crackled over the fire. When it was ready, the men sat down to eat.

"This is about as quiet an evening as I have known," said Smith. "It is so peaceful that you wouldn't think an Indian or a wild animal was anywhere near."

The evening air did indeed seem peaceful. Zenas, through with his supper, stood leaning against the rocky face of the bluff. He thought of the village where he had grown up back east in Pennsylvania. It was peaceful, too, but in a different way. He liked the west when it was spring or summer, but the winters were bad. When the wind and the wild animals tried to outdo each other in howling on a winter night, he wished he were home. He had been away for a year, but it seemed forever.

Smith and Fully were lying on their backs about twelve feet away from Zenas, back from the bluff. Their eyes were closed.

"Do you think we should be going back to where we left the other trappers?" Zenas asked.

Smith opened his eyes. He was about to answer when he suddenly jumped to his feet.

"Zenas!" he yelled. "A bear! On top of the bluff!"

Fully jumped up, too. He stopped just long enough to see the bear above Zenas' head, some fifteen feet up. Then he, and Smith, too, turned to run.

Zenas swung about and looked up. There, ready to leap down on him, was a huge grizzly bear. For an instant that seemed to go on and on, Zenas stared at the great beast. What should he do? Should he run? No — to do so would bring the bear leaping down upon him with his crushing weight. When a man turned his back to a bear, he usually lost his life. The grizzly bear of the west seemed held off, for some reason, if a man could keep his face to him and not make a sudden move.

Zenas turned his head just enough to see that his gun was leaning against the bluff about an arm's length away. Without turning or looking away from the bear, he called, "Smith! Fully! Get your rifles ready! I'm going to shoot."

Smith and Fully had turned back almost as soon as they had begun to run away. They knew that the bear might forget Zenas and take after them if they ran. Keeping an eye on the bear, each man got his rifle and checked to see that it was loaded.

Zenas heard a snarl above his head.

The bear was drawing back, getting ready to leap. Quickly, Zenas raised his gun and pointed it at the bear's chest. He pulled the trigger just as the bear moved forward.

Two other shots rang out at almost the same instant. The three men jumped back as the huge animal came falling down. It hit the ground with a great thud.

Zenas and the two other trappers were reloading their guns. If the animal was only wounded, they would need to be ready. But the bear did not move, and they stepped near.

"All three of us hit him," said Zenas. "It is hard to tell which bullet killed him — or perhaps it was the fall. At any rate, we will have bear meat for breakfast."

They were soon busy skinning and butchering the bear. Two men worked while the third watched the bluff to be sure that another bear did not come visiting. The smell of the buffalo meat cooking could draw it or other wild animals to the bluff.

The peacefulness of the evening was gone. "A trapper's life is not peaceful for long," Zenas thought as he lay down at last to sleep.

A day or two later, the three men went back to the camp of the rest of their party.

"Any word from Gant?" they called out as they came near.

The fifteen men waiting there looked discouraged. "No sign of him or of the other parties trapping for him," they said.

The next day, there was excitement in the camp.

"Look!" a scout called. "A large party of men coming this way! It looks like a pack train."

A man on horseback rode out ahead of the great body of men and horses coming near. He headed towards the camp of the trappers.

"It is Mr. Fitzpatrick!" someone called out. The man who was riding toward the trappers looked as if he had lived outdoors for many years, as indeed he had. He was in charge of the Rocky Mountain Fur Company's work in the western part of the Rockies. He had been in the mountains for a long time.

"Hello!" he called. "How have you done since we met last fall?"

"Not so well," answered Mr. Stephens. "We lost our horses, and had a great deal of trouble. But we do have some furs to trade, and are waiting for Captain Gant to come with supplies."

"Gant!" said Fitzpatrick. "Haven't you heard? He

gave up finding you and went on south. Kit Carson just left us to join him. But his company has gone out of business in St. Louis."

Zenas and the other men of Stephens' party looked at each other. This was all they needed to add to their troubles. Gant would not be coming back this way at all.

But Fitzpatrick had an idea. "Come to the big rendezvous at Pierre's Hole—up where the Snake River begins," he said. "Ride along with William Sublette. That is his pack train you see over there, taking supplies from St. Louis to the rendezvous."

The discouraged men brightened. That was the answer — the Rocky Mountain Fur Company would buy their furs, and they could get the supplies they needed. It would mean good times, too. A "rendezvous" was a big meeting of all the trappers who could get to it, and it lasted about three weeks.

TO THE RENDEZVOUS

And so it was that Zenas set off for the big rendez-vous of 1832 at Pierre's Hole.

They came by twos, by tens, and by hundreds. They came from the north where the Missouri River began. They came from near the Great Salt Lake to the south, and from the hunting grounds in the Rockies to the east and to the west. Indians and whites, "company" men and free trappers, all made their way with their packs of furs to Pierre's Hole in eastern Idaho.

All along the seventy-mile stretch of the Teton River, trappers were gathering. Indian tepees and skin shelters not large enough to cover a man were set up. There were noisy greetings, the singing of songs, and the telling of tales that grew taller with each telling. Now and then there was a fist fight between two rough moun-tain men. This was Pierre's Hole at rendezvous time.

The trappers were waiting for the most important men of all—those who brought the trading goods from St. Louis. In that city, far away, Captain William Sublet-te had gathered sixty men to help him with the long

line of pack horses he needed to carry the goods. They walked westward, following the Missouri River past frontier towns and pioneer farms until they came to the last town of all—Independence, Missouri.

"We'll give the men a chance to enjoy themselves here in Independence for a few days," Captain Sublette said to his partner, Robert Campbell. "We can buy some more mules here, and some of the goods coming by steamboat."

Independence was near the big bend of the Missouri River, and a little east of the place where the Kansas River emptied into the Missouri. A trail led west along the Kansas River, but there would be no more towns and few farms from the time they turned onto that trail.

The men made camp near the little town. Camping alongside them was a group of about forty men who did not look like trappers and frontiersmen.

"I wonder who those fellows are," Sublette said to Campbell. "They look as if they've been traveling a long time, but I would guess they were from the east, not the west."

Just then one of the men came walking towards them. He held out his hand as he said, "How do you do, gentlemen. My name is Nathaniel J. Wyeth."

Sublette and Campbell introduced themselves. They soon learned that Mr. Wyeth was from Boston, and that he was the leader of the party of travelers.

"We are going to the Columbia River in Oregon," he told the fur-company men. "There we shall start a salmon fishery, as I am told the river has plenty of fish."

Captain Sublette and Mr. Campbell looked at Mr. Wyeth in surprise.

"Do you know how far you still must go? It is about two thousand miles from here, and through the wildest, roughest of mountains after you cross the great plains," Sublette said.

Mr. Wyeth did not look upset.

"We have come over a thousand miles already," he said, "and things have gone quite well. We came by steamboat most of the way. I have bought wagons and teams for the overland trip. Can we not simply travel on from here to the Pacific Ocean in them?"

Robert Campbell stared at the man from the east. Wagons! There were places on the trail where even a pack horse had trouble getting through. A fur-company man named Captain Bonneville was trying out wagons to get to the rendezvous. But to cross the Rocky Mountains in them! This man knew nothing of the swift rivers

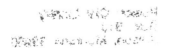

to be crossed, the narrow mountain trails, and probably very little of how to care for himself on the open plains where no white man had yet built a house. Some of his men did not even have rifles! How would they protect themselves from Indians? How would they get food?

"Mr. Wyeth," he said, "you and your men had better travel with us. We know what is ahead. You will never make it alone. Our hunters will help you get food, and we will teach you the ways of the west."

So it was that when the pack train set out again, Mr. Wyeth's men went along. The men of the west showed them how to choose a camping place, how to use a rifle, and many other things needed just to stay alive.

By the end of the first week on the trail across the plains, Mr. Wyeth said, "I can see now how foolish we were to think of starting out alone, Mr. Campbell and Captain Sublette. We will always be grateful to you."

The pack train moved on slowly. Each day found the travelers from ten to twenty miles farther along the trail. Westward they went, and then north to the valley of the Platte River in what is now Nebraska. By the time they had started westward again following the Platte, the easterners were beginning to look like frontiersmen.

One day, a lone rider was seen coming toward them

51

from the west. The scouts riding ahead of the long pack train watched him until they could tell if the rider were white or Indian.

"Why, it is Mr. Fitzpatrick!" one of them called. "I'd know him anywhere. He rides as if he were born in the saddle."

Thomas Fitzpatrick had been in the mountains for years. He was a partner in the Rocky Mountain Fur Company, and the rendezvous at Pierre's Hole was under his direction.

"Hello!" he called out as he neared the scouts. "I came to see if you were getting anywhere near the rendezvous. Men are waiting there for Sublette to come with the trading goods."

Sublette and Campbell had ridden forward to meet him. "Good to see you, Fitzpatrick. How has the take of beaver been this year?"

"Most of the trappers had a good hunt," said Fitzpatrick. "It is going to be a big rendezvous."

Fitzpatrick joined the pack train and headed back the way he had just come. The men and horses reached the mouth of the Sweetwater River where it empties into the Platte. From then on, they saw other parties of trappers heading for the great rendezvous. Usually, the small parties joined the big group. Kit Carson was with one of the small groups, but when he heard that Captain Gant was somewhere to the south, he left to join him. Right after that, Zenas Leonard's party decided to go with Sublette, too. By then there were at least one hundred fifty men riding together.

It was a day or so after he had talked to Zenas' party that Thomas Fitzpatrick grew tired of the slowness of the pack train.

"I am going to ride on ahead," he said to Sublette. "I have been thinking about what might be going on at Pierre's Hole. If I am not there, the traders from the American Fur Company might be buying the best of the furs. I will be there when you get there."

He took a supply of meat and his blankets and rode on ahead. The men of the pack train watched him set off alone.

Another week went by with little happening other than more miles traveled toward the rendezvous. Then came the morning that marked the beginning of trouble.

Soon after the day's ride began, one of the lead horsemen called out, "Hold back! We are in quicksand!"

The horses were having great trouble in lifting

their feet. Quickly, the men turned the rest of the train to the right.

"Whoa! Easy, boy!" men called to their horses. The poor, frightened animals tried to get a foothold and turn about. There was a great noise of horses whinnying and men shouting. One pack horse sank so that only his head was above the quicksand. It took a good deal of pulling to get him out.

"We'll have to go quite a way off the trail to get clear of this," said Campbell.

They at last found their way around the quicksand, and had gone a short distance when it began to grow dark.

"Since we are in grizzly bear country now, we had better choose a good high spot for our camp tonight," said Robert Campbell.

The wind whipped across the plains and around the rocks that night. Dust blew into the men's faces as they tried to sleep. They had reached a part of the country where there was little grass growing.

"Hunting isn't very good here," said Campbell. "We will need to travel faster if we are to have enough to eat."

They began the climb into the mountains, and went

through woods of fir, pine and cedar. On and on they went, each day getting a little nearer to Pierre's Hole, and each day more thankful for the little meat the hunter could shoot for them.

They left the valley of the Sweetwater, and headed for Wind River valley. They followed it until they were ready to go westward through a mountain pass. The going was rough, and the men were growing very tired.

Nathaniel Wyeth rode alongside of Captain Sublette.

"I see now that we were foolish to think we could ever make this trip alone," he said. "If it were not for you and your men, every one of us easterners would have died by now."

"The trip is almost over now," said Campbell. "At least the first part of it is. After the rendezvous, there will be a party of trappers heading for the Columbia River, and you can go on with them."

That night, the camp was quiet as soon as darkness came. The horses had been tied near a patch of grass alongside a stream. The evening meal had been cooked, and the fires allowed to die down. They learned something that night which taught them to travel away from their telltale campfires before going to sleep..

About midnight, the camp was suddenly awakened by Indian war whoops and yells. A shower of rifle shots hit the tents.

Tiredness was forgotten in the minutes that followed. The sounds of horses' hoof beats and excited whinnies mixed with the cries of white men and Indians. But the attack was over almost as soon as it began.

"That was close—too close," said William Sublette as he pulled an arrow from his tent. He examined it carefully. "Blackfeet. I knew we were getting into Blackfoot country, but I didn't think any were around. We'll have to march on after our evening meal, and post a guard from here on."

"Why did they leave so quickly?" asked Mr. Wyeth.

"They saw how big a company we had," answered Campbell. "I think this attack was meant to scare us, and to get some of our horses. We'd better look around to see if anyone was hurt, and how many horses they took."

No one had been hurt, but several horses had broken loose and had been rushed away by the Indians. One mule had been wounded.

"We were lucky. We could all have been killed in our sleep," Sublette said. "I am sorry to lose the horses, but better to lose horses than men."

No one slept any more that night. Packs were put together and tied to the pack animals. Riding horses were saddled. The whole camp moved on towards the pass in the mountains, more watchful than ever before.

That was the last of their troubles on the way. But when at last they entered the long valley called "Pierre's Hole," it was to find out that Fitzpatrick had not arrived.

"He should have been here ten days ago," said Sublette. "Something has gone wrong!"

FITZPATRICK'S ADVENTURE

Thomas Fitzpatrick did not mind traveling alone. He felt free as he rode ahead of the slow pack train. His horse took him quickly ahead from the Sweetwater River valley through a pass in the Rocky Mountains to the valley of the Green River. From there he would go northward to Pierre's Hole.

This trail was new to Fitzpatrick. When, on the fourth day, the weather became cloudy and dull he had to stop to decide which was the right direction. He could not get through the heavy growth of trees and brush in some places. Many, many times he had to turn to go around great rocks. By the sixth day, he could see no landmarks he knew.

It was sunny the next day, and Fitzpatrick could keep heading northward with little trouble. But travel was slow and hard, and he knew he was not on the trail to Pierre's Hole. As the sun dropped low to the west, he chose a place to eat his supper. He turned his horse loose to graze, took a chunk of dried meat from his pack, and sat down with his back against a rock.

"Ah,—it feels good to rest," he said aloud. He found himself nodding as he chewed the dry meat.

Suddenly he heard something that brought him wide awake. It was the sound of claws scrambling onto the big rocks behind him. He jumped to his feet and turned around. There, coming toward him, was a big grizzly bear.

"I'll hold my ground," thought Fitzpatrick. He knew he could not outrun the bear. Sometimes bears had been known to turn away from men who stood still and looked right at them.

When the bear was six feet from the trapper, he stopped and rose to a standing position on his hind legs. Fitzpatrick kept his eyes on the bear's face. Seconds passed as the bear stood ready to attack and the man stared at the great jaws above him. The bear's long, curled claws seemed ready to tear the man open.

Then, suddenly, the bear came down to stand on four feet, turned, and ran back the way he had come.

"I wonder what made him change his mind," Fitzpatrick thought. He felt free for a moment. Then he knew he must be ready if the bear came back.

"I must get away from here," was his only thought.

He ran towards his horse. The horse had caught the smell of the bear and was uneasy. He saw his master running towards him. Coming around the rocks and towards them both was the bear.

With a great whinny, the horse jumped away just as Fitzpatrick was about to jump onto his back. The man fell to the ground. He heard the bear coming closer, and his fright gave him the strength to jump quickly to his feet.

"A-a-a-a-rugh!" It was Fitzpatrick, playing the bear's own game. He growled almost as fiercely as the bear and rushed forward to meet the beast.

Startled at the strange way this man was acting, the bear stopped in his tracks. He watched for a moment as the man continued to come toward him, making horrible noises. Then he turned and ran back to a safe distance. He stopped as he passed the rock near where Fitzpatrick had been eating and took the rest of the chunk of meat.

Fitzpatrick's heart was pounding. He ran behind a large, low rock while the bear was busy with the chunk of meat. Carefully he crept towards the place where his gun leaned against a rock, keeping the rocks between him and the bear.

He gripped the gun. Now he was ready to fight. The gun was loaded and ready. Fitzpatrick slowly rose and looked over the rocks to find the bear.

The old grizzly was sniffing about to find any food he might have missed. Just as he raised his head to find what he thought would make a fine dinner, the "dinner" pulled the trigger on the rifle. The bear rose onto his hind legs with a fearful noise. Then down he fell.

"That got old grizzly," said Fitzpatrick. He reloaded and then walked towards the animal, keeping his rifle ready.

But his one shot had been true. The bear lay still.

"Instead of you having me for dinner, I'll have you," Fitzpatrick said. He took his knife from his belt, cut away the bear's coat, and took the best cut of meat. He built a fire and cooked the meat on a stick. But as he ate, he kept a sharp ear and a watchful eye for any other of the bear family.

His horse was still upset from his fright, although Fitzpatrick had caught and tied him while the meat cooked. He whinnied and moved about restlessly. As soon as Fitzpatrick had finished eating, he packed his belongings and got on the horse. They went on two or three miles farther and camped for the night beside a stream.

In the morning, Fitzpatrick made ready to leave.

He started along the bank of the creek, winding his way between the trees and around rocks. It was almost noon when he entered a valley. The creek turned about a great cliff and then left the valley again. On all sides, mountains rose from the valley floor.

"This is a place I've never been before," he thought. His horse pawed restlessly as Fitzpatrick looked around. Then the horse's ears went forward as he listened. He stiffened and a wild look came into his eyes.

"What's wrong, boy?" Fitzpatrick asked. Then he knew the answer, for he heard the sound of an arrow whizzing by his head. He looked back quickly. There, behind him, blocking the way out of the valley, was a group of young warriors on horseback.

"Go, boy!" cried Fitzpatrick, and he dug his heels into his horse's sides.

The horse took off and ran as he had never run before. He bounded over ditches, stones, logs and

brush. He ran the full length of the valley, and then there was no place to go but upward. The climb was steep and rough, and the good horse began to stumble. Behind him, Fitzpatrick heard the yelling Indians draw closer.

"Come on, boy," he urged his horse. "Run for your life—and mine!"

But the poor horse was too tired to go on up the steep mountain side. Fitzpatrick turned his head and saw that the Indians were having trouble, too, but they were closer than they had been before. He jumped from his horse.

"Good-by, old friend," he said, and patted his horse's side. Then he left him and ran on up the mountain. As he climbed, his side began to pain him. His heart pounded and he could hardly breathe.

He moved in behind some brush. From the sounds, he knew the Indians had left their horses, too, and were coming after him on foot.

"I must find a hiding place," he thought, and went this way and that, looking for a spot where he might not be found.

He heard the calls of joy when his horse was found. Fitzpatrick hoped for a moment that they might give up the chase for him and be satisfied with the horse. But in a few minutes he knew they had started the search again.

But those minutes had given him the time he needed. He had found a very thick clump of brush growing right in front of a steep-sided rock. He pushed in behind the bushes. Then it was that he saw the opening in the rock. It had not shown from outside the bushes.

"Luck is with me," he thought. He found the opening just large enough to crawl into. It widened as he went in, and the space inside was large enough for him to seat himself quite comfortably.

"I would guess that a bear curls up in here in the winter," he thought. "I am mighty glad he is not at home today."

Then he heard an Indian coming close. Would he see the shadow — the darkness that marked the hole in the rocks? Fitzpatrick held his breath as the Indian came alongside the bushes. He let it out again — the Indian had gone on by without noticing.

The Indians passed and re-passed Fitzpatrick's hiding place. They called to each other from time to time. Then at last the calls grew fainter.

"They've given up. I'll use the little daylight that

is left to find my way over this mountain," thought Fitz-patrick. He crawled out of his hiding place. Slowly he worked his way around the bushes. He was about to stand up when he heard a sound that sent him backing towards his hole in the rocks. He stayed outside just long enough to see that four of the Indians were coming back.

"They've remembered this place and have come back to look," Fitzpatrick thought. He pulled himself well back into the hole. He hardly dared breathe as the Indians came nearer. They passed not six feet from the hole through which he had crawled, but they did not look in. On they went about fifty feet farther, Fitzpatrick thought from the sounds. He heard them pulling aside some brush, and guessed there might be another hole like the one he was in. The tone of their voices told him they were disappointed. They came towards his hiding place again and went on down the mountain side.

Fitzpatrick stayed inside for a long time. He heard them call their horses and guessed they were riding back down into the valley, leading Fitzpatrick's horse.

Night had come when Fitzpatrick left his hole again.

"I'll try to find my way down the mountain and pass

the Indian camp in the darkness," he thought. "If I can find the creek again, I'll follow it out of this trap."

He made his way slowly downward. The night was dark, and the trees added to the darkness. He felt his way along. It seemed the mountain side would never end when at last he felt the ground become more level.

Fitzpatrick walked on in what he hoped was the right direction. The trip down the mountain had taken him many hours, and already a faint streak of light showed that sunrise was not far off. He heard the water running in the creek, and at the same instant found that he was walking into the Indians' camp. As quickly as he could without making a sound, he turned about and hurried back to the mountain side. He used the time before full daylight to find himself another hiding place.

When he was sure he had not left a trail that would bring the Indians to him, he made himself as comfortable as he could and went to sleep. He was hungry, but there was no way to get food until he was free from the Indians.

In the middle of the morning he was awakened by the yells of the young Indians. One of them must have seen his footprints, and they knew he was near.

They searched for an hour or two, while Fitzpatrick hardly dared breathe. Then they tired of the search and looked for something else to do.

They went back down into the valley. Fitzpatrick crawled to the opening of his hiding place and looked down. He watched as all afternoon the Indians raced their horses against the prize they had captured from him.

"That's it, boy—show them you are the best horse of all," Fitzpatrick said aloud as he watched his horse beat three Indian ponies, one after another. By the fourth race, his horse was beginning to tire. The fresh Indian pony beat him.

"He'll drop in his tracks," Fitzpatrick thought angrily as he saw them getting ready for a fifth race. This race was easily won by the other horse. Then at last they seemed satisfied!

The hours went by and darkness came at last. Once more, Fitzpatrick started the trip to freedom. This time he knew where the Indian camp lay along the creek.

He circled the camp, moving quietly and slowly so as not to waken even a dog.

By morning, he had safely circled the camp and

found the place where the creek left the valley. He was only a short way down the creek beyond the valley when daylight and sounds of the Indians coming near made him hide again.

He was lying perfectly still in the brush along the creek when he heard a hunting party coming from the camp. He watched as they rode by him—not twenty feet away. On Fitzpatrick's own horse rode an Indian who looked as if he might be the chief.

"How I'd like to run out there, push him off, and get on my horse and ride away," thought Fitzpatrick. But he knew that to try would be foolish.

He slept awhile. He heard the party of Indians coming back. When they had passed, he pulled at the plants growing near him to find roots he might eat, for hunger was making him weak. When the shadows deepened, he crawled to the creek and drank of the water. Then, after looking carefully about, he set out to put distance between him and the Indians.

He followed the creek until it emptied into the river.

"If I cross the river, I will run less chance of running into the Indians," he thought. He spent the hours that were left of that night making a raft of driftwood.

He tied the logs together with tough vines. When the raft was ready, he laid on it his pack which had been on his back. In it was his blanket and the few things he used when fixing meals. He set his rifle and shot pouch on the raft beside him and pushed off with a pole.

The raft had taken him almost to the other side when suddenly all was lost. The shadows of the trees and rocks on the far bank made it hard to see. Just as Fitzpatrick thought he had made the crossing safely, the raft hit a sharp rock. It fell apart. Man, gun, blanket and all were thrown into the river.

Fitzpatrick reached wildly to find the gun. Other than his knife, it was his only means of protecting himself and getting food. In the darkness, the current swept it away. Fitzpatrick had to give up and fight the current to get himself to the shore.

He climbed out, dripping and unhappy. Slowly, he picked his way along the river bank, afraid to go on, but more afraid to stop. Wildcats, wolves, grizzly bears —any of them could easily kill him. He felt for his knife —thank heavens, it was still in his belt!

When morning came, Fitzpatrick dug with his knife for roots to keep him alive. Two days went by. He learned to know which roots were easiest to eat. He had found one with a better taste than the others, and on the second evening he was digging for it when a sound brought him to his feet.

"Gr-r-r-r-r-r!"

He stood up and swung about. There, coming down the slope was a wolf. No—it was a whole pack of wolves. Fitzpatrick used the little strength he had to get himself to the nearest strong tree and up into the branches. The wolves tore at the ground about the tree and leaped into it. For a while, Fitzpatrick was sure they would tear it out by the roots. All through the night, he clung to the branches of the tree. When the wolves had at last given up, he was afraid to come down for fear they would find him in the dark.

It was at the end of the fourth day after his escape that he came upon what was left of a buffalo that wolves had killed and eaten. He scraped the bones with his knife to get any scraps of meat that were on them. Then came the long, slow job of starting a fire without matches. He blew at the tiny sparks that at last came as he rubbed sticks together. The dry pine needles and leaves he had gathered took fire.

"I don't think I could have waited much longer,"

he thought. "I'd have eaten the meat raw—but I can enjoy it when it is cooked."

He felt like a king as he ate the first meat he had had in over a week—since the night he had killed the grizzly. But it was the last he was to have for another week. As he went on down the river, even the roots became harder to find. Each day he grew weaker.

"If only I could get to the mouth of this river," he thought. "I am sure it runs into the Snake River. Then someone might find me—someone from the rendezvous."

"Go on—must go on," he found himself saying aloud. But his body would not obey. He fell into a deep sleep.

"I will die here," he thought. "Forgive my sins—"

"Here he is! It's Fitzpatrick!"

Three trappers jumped from their horses and ran to where a fourth man was leaning over the thinnest man they had ever seen.

They made him drink and eat a very little. Then the men made a stretcher with poles and a blanket. They carried the starving man on the stretcher between a pair of horses, and made their way back to the rendezvous.

Fitzpatrick was put to bed and cared for. After a

few days of rest, he was able to join the other men. Then the real business of the rendezvous began. Trading went on and men enjoyed food they had not had for a year. With all the ammunition and most of the things they would need for the next year set aside, they set about enjoying themselves.

Then, one by one, the hunting parties packed up enough gun powder and shot, coffee, sugar and flour to last until the next rendezvous, a year ahead. New beading and ornaments were sewed to buckskin leggings and moccasins. New feathers were tied to horses' bridles and to rifles. Then, gay and cheerful, they set off for their chosen hunting grounds, and for no-one-knew-what adventures.

"See you next year! Have a good hunt!" they called. The hundreds in Pierre's Hole became tens. A few days more, and they, too, were gone. Fitzpatrick, Sublette and Campbell saw that the furs were packed onto the pack horses and mules. Fitzpatrick went back to the mountains; Sublette and Campbell started the long journey back to St. Louis.

Pierre's Hole was quiet again. The big rendezvous was over.

KIT CARSON, MAN OF COURAGE

At the time Davy Crockett was hunting bears in Tennessee, Kit Carson was growing up near the little frontier town of Franklin, Missouri. Kit ran away to go west when he was a boy of seventeen.

He got a job with a wagon train going to Santa Fe, and made his first trip into the great west. From then on, he led the life of a trapper and hunter.

By 1837, he had been in the west for eleven years, and he knew the ways of the wilderness as well as any man. Many were the grizzly bears he had faced. His meetings with unfriendly Indians had usually ended with Kit the winner. When other men said, "Let's give up and go back," Kit usually was planning for another adventure.

For years, Blackfeet had been giving the trappers a great deal of trouble as they trapped in the streams near Yellowstone and upper Missouri Rivers. But during the winter of 1836-37 they had been quiet.

"You know why, don't you?" Kit said when a newly arrived trapper asked about it. "The white men brought smallpox to the Indians. The Blackfeet went north to try to get away from it. Even so, I hear many of their warriors died."

Kit and some other trappers had gone up into northern Montana trying to find the beaver. Now they were looking up one of the side streams for "beaver signs"—gnawed branches floating on the streams and the tracks of the little animal.

Kit said, "There are plenty of beaver signs here, but there are other signs, too. Blackfeet traveled along here, and not very long ago."

"Blackfeet!" said his leader, whose name was Fontenelle. "I hoped we would finish our spring trapping without meeting them."

Each day, the trappers looked for the trail of the Indians. Each day, Kit was sure the trappers were nearer to them.

Then one day he said, "Captain, the Blackfeet are only one day ahead of us. We'll come upon their camp any time now. Either we will have to go to another stream, or we will have to fight them soon."

"Trapping is good here," said Mr. Fontenelle. "I'd like to know how many Indians there are."

"Well," said Kit, "I'll go find out."

Fontenelle looked at the small wiry man with the courage of a mountain lion.

"All right," he said, "but take a few men with you."

Soon Kit and five other trappers were ready to go. They set out on the well-marked trail of the Indians. They had gone only a little way when they saw enough to report back.

"There are about fifty Indians in the camp, Captain," said Kit. "They are rounding up their animals and getting ready to move on."

"Fine," said Fontenelle. "We will work along behind them."

"Well, Captain," said Kit, "I'm not for that at all. We might be killed in our sleep if they learn we are near. The Blackfeet have stolen our horses and done everything they could to hurt us. Now we have just as much right to hunt here as they have. I'm for showing them up."

"What do you mean to do, Kit?" asked Fontenelle.

"There are one hundred of us here. I'll take—say, forty men. That will leave plenty here to come to help us if we need them. We'll take the Indians by surprise and scare them away for good."

Some of the men shook their heads. "Better not go

looking for trouble," they said.

But forty men offered to go with Kit, and they set out. They reached the Indian camp without being discovered.

Kit placed his men in a half circle about the camp. At a signal, they all fired. Ten Indians fell. The others, taken by surprise, hurried to get into protected places.

"Forward!" yelled Kit.

The Indians were not ready for the charge. They had just time to pick up rifles and ammunition.

"Look at them run!" yelled one of the trappers. But as soon as they could find good spots from which to fire, the Indians began to fight. Kit and his men made them move back again and again. For three hours the fighting went on, and it looked as if the trappers would win.

Then bad news was passed up the line to Kit.

"We are almost out of ammunition."

The trappers' firing slowed down, and the Indians knew their chance had come. They began to charge. This time the trappers had to back away.

"To your horses, men!" ordered Carson. "Back to camp for ammunition!"

The men ran back through the woods to where their horses were tied at the other side of the Indian camp. Most of them reached the animals ahead of Kit and were quickly on them and riding away.

A horrible yell came to Kit's ears as he jumped on his horse's back. The Indians were charging after them, as fast as they could come.

Kit's horse ran alongside the horse of a man named Cotton.

"Come on, Cotton! We've got to move fast!" yelled Kit.

Just then, Cotton's horse stumbled over a rock. The horse fell to the ground with a thud.

"Help! Help!" yelled Cotton.

Kit turned to see what had happened. There was Cotton, on the ground with one leg held down by the kicking horse.

"I'll help you, Cotton!" he called. "Hold on, we'll get you free!" Kit jumped from his horse and ran towards Cotton. He tried to get the horse up onto his feet so that Cotton could pull his leg free. As he worked he heard, altogether too close, the terrible cry of the Indian on the warpath.

He looked up. There, tomahawks raised and ready

for the kill, were six Indian braves running toward him and Cotton.

Kit wasted no time. "Try to get up now, Cotton," he yelled. Forward he ran, right toward the charging Indians.

"Crack!" Kit fired and the bullet whistled forward. Five Indians stopped as the sixth one fell to the ground. Kit reloaded and charged on ahead. But his next shot was at the Indians' backs, for they had turned to run. Kit Carson was not a man they cared to face— even at five to one!

Quickly, Kit turned to see how Cotton was getting along. Luckily, he had been able to get himself and his horse both on their feet, and he was riding away. Kit looked about for his own horse.

"Whoa!" he yelled. But the frightened animal was running after Cotton's horse as fast as he could go.

"Whoa!" Kit yelled again. But his horse was not waiting for anyone. Kit looked over his shoulder. The Indians had stopped and were turning back to attack again.

"Now I am in a fine fix," Kit thought. His last bullet was in his rifle.

"Carson!" came a yell. "Up here with me!"

One of Kit's men had seen what had happened. He turned and rode quickly towards Kit, slowing down just enough for Kit to jump up behind him. Then his horse hurried on and carried the two men safely to the trappers' camp.

"Get ready for another charge!" the order went. Each man in the camp hurried to get a good supply of ammunition. They had just moved out from the camp a short way when they met the Indian fire again. The Indians had taken positions behind rocks.

"Bang! Bang! Bang!" Rifle after rifle rang out. Bullets flew in both directions. But the trappers were now one hundred strong. Some of them found ways to get around the rocks where the Indians hid, following Kit's lead.

"Come on, boys! We'll get them out of their holes!" he yelled, and charged forward. Again, there were other men ready to follow. The Indians had to run back to other hiding places.

"Show your face, Blackfoot!" a trapper would yell. An Indian would pop up just long enough to fire in the direction from which the yell came. Then the trapper would run forward with his loaded rifle. The Indian, left without a charge in his rifle, had no choice but to run to a new place of safety.

"After them, men!" yelled Kit, "We've got them running now! Scare them off so far that they won't be able to find their way back!"

But the Indians were not ready to give up the fight. They met fire with fire, and some of the trappers were wounded. Then the turning point came.

This time the Indians were the ones to run out of ammunition. With no bullets left, they had to run to save their lives.

When he saw what had happened, Kit ran back to camp for his horse. Others followed him as usual. They leaped onto their horses, although they were all tired from five hours of fighting.

After the fleeing Indians they rode, yelling as fiercely as any Indian ever had yelled. They picked off each Indian they could find, until at last none were foolish enough to come out of hiding.

That night, the Indians who had lived through the battle packed up the last of their goods and rode away. Kit's courage had won the hunting ground for the trappers.

In days to come, miners and ranchers were to take over the wild land. But it was men like Kit Carson who cleared the way for others to follow.

BUFFALO HUNTER IN THE MAKING

Years went by. Mr. Wyeth's idea that men could go to the Pacific Ocean by wagon was proven to be not so foolish after all. It did not work for him, but passes were found through the mountains and trails were widened. From 1843 on, great trains of covered wagons cut across the plains and followed trails to Oregon and to California.

Kit Carson and the other trappers found it harder each year to find enough beavers to make their trip pay. The great days of the fur trade ended, and the aging trappers settled down at last. But through their traveling about, the "face" of the west had become known.

Although the beavers were gone, another animal was roaming the west in greater number every year. A new group of hunters came, hunters whose ways of working were much different from those of the beaver trappers. The day of the buffalo hunter had come. Boys who went west for adventure, as Kit Carson had done so long ago, now looked to buffalo hunting for excitement and a way to earn a living.

One such young man was John Cook. One day, he found the camp of an old buffalo hunter named Charlie Hart.

"What makes you think you can hunt buffalo, young man?" asked Charlie.

"I've been working as a skinner all fall," answered John. "I camped with some people who did a little buffalo hunting. They showed me how to skin and butcher the animals. I earned my gun and outfit that way." John rubbed his left hand along the barrel of his gun—a Sharp's 44 caliber rifle. He smiled proudly. Then he added, "Of course, what I'd really like to do, Mr. Hart, is to hunt buffalo. But I'll take a skinner's job if you want me."

"Might be you can get a chance to do a little hunting," said Charlie. "But I need a good skinner. It takes several skinners to keep up with me. I can do all the hunting we can take care of." Charlie smiled, and young John knew that he was telling the truth. Charlie Hart, six-feet tall and like wire, was known as one of the best buffalo hunters of the west.

"I'll pay you twenty-five cents for each buffalo you skin," said Charlie. "Think it over."

John did not need to think it over long. He had soon made up his mind to join Charlie Hart's men for the big hunt. When the time came for the hunt to start, he was on hand with three other men and a boy of seventeen. The five of them would take care of Charlie's camp and the animals he killed.

A few days after New Year's Day of 1875, the little band left their camp in the "panhandle" of Texas. John drove a two-horse team pulling a light wagon loaded with bedding, ammunition, extra guns and and other supplies. One of the other men drove the wagon with the camping outfit and food in it. The third man drove a heavy wagon with six yoke of oxen. This would be needed for moving the great piles of buffalo skins they planned to get. The boy, whose name was Frank, and Charlie rode horseback.

They headed south, killing a few buffalo along the way. After traveling about ten days, they suddenly found themselves in the feeding grounds of great herds of buffalo.

Charlie took his field glasses and rode to a high spot.

"This is it!" he cried as he came back to the wagons. "I can see ten thousand buffalo from up there!

We'll choose a spot for our camp, and hunt from here."

They found a place where there was a spring of fresh water, good grass for their horses and oxen, and plenty of wood for fires.

"We'll start the hunt tomorrow," said Charlie when the camp had been set up.

He rode out at eight o'clock the next morning with his big 50 caliber gun and a supply of ammunition. A short time later, John and one of the men, Warren Dockum, set out together with one of the wagons and a team.

They followed Charlie's trail, and before long they found where the shooting had begun. They pulled the wagon alongside the first of a line of dead buffaloes stretching out ahead of them.

"He's killed us a day's work already," said Warren. "Look ahead, there! Buffaloes lying waiting for us as far as we can see."

As John jumped down from the wagon and pulled his knife from his belt, he thought of the first day he had worked as a buffalo skinner. He had skinned ten of the animals, and had been so tired he could hardly get back to camp. He would have to do much better than that today!

"Hook that chain onto the buffalo's front left leg," Warren called. John picked up the chain which hung from the back axle of the wagon and did as he was told. Before he had it fastened, Warren had made the first cut to "peel" the hide from the animal.

In a moment or two, it was time to move the team forward a few feet to move the big, heavy animal. The skin was pulled back to the backbone as the two men worked to loosen it with their knives. Then the wagon was moved on again, and the skin was pulled down the other side of the buffalo. They cut it free at the legs and tail and the job was finished.

"One done!" called Warren as he threw the hide into the wagon. They jumped onto the seat and moved quickly on to the next buffalo, leaving the meat and all of the first buffalo lying there. They would take only enough buffalo hump roasts back to camp to supply them with food.

That first day, John and Warren skinned thirty-three buffaloes. Charlie had hunted for only two hours, and sixty-three of the big animals lay dead—more than his men could care for in a day.

The next morning work began much earlier. It was harder to skin a buffalo which had lain overnight, and John and Warren worked as fast as they could to catch up. The third man, Cyrus, had also gone out skinning.

After a few days, Warren was needed to help Frank care for the skins at the camp. Each skin had to be "pegged out" to stretch and dry it in good shape. Little holes were cut through the hide all around the edges, and pegs were put through the holes and driven into the ground. After three days, the skin had to be turned over and re-pegged, flesh side up, scraped and worked over. When the skins were dry, they were sorted as to kind and stacked in great piles, which grew to be eight feet high.

Caring for the skins was the work of the camp-keeper, along with reloading of the rifle shells and cooking the meals. Frank and Warren usually did this work. John had to go out alone to do the skinning.

Day after day, John went out to the open plains following the dead buffalo path which Charlie left behind him. Each day he became a little tougher. But each day also found him growing a little more tired of skinning buffaloes. At the end of the day, he checked over his rifle carefully and, often he went out for an hour or two of hunting.

Elk and deer came to the near-by river to drink. Their meat was a pleasant change when the men grew tired of buffalo humps, and John enjoyed the chance to hunt for them. Soon after they made camp, he had shot a wild turkey, remembering how good they had tasted back in Missouri. But these turkeys were bitter tasting. After one meal of them, John knew why the birds walked about so close to camp.

"They know that no man in his right mind would eat them, and they are perfectly safe," John said.

About the time that John began to wonder if he and Cyrus would ever catch up with Charlie, they found the daily kill becoming smaller. One day, they rode a long time before finding any dead animals. From then on, the hunting became poorer and poorer.

"Let's take a day off," Charlie said one morning. "Then we'll pack up and move on to a new hunting ground. I think the buffalo have gone farther north now that spring is coming."

"A day off?" asked Cyrus. "Fine, Charlie. How about seeing if we can track down that wildcat?"

The wildcat had been seen around the camp, but always at a time when the men could not follow it. Charlie, John and Cyrus set out to track it down. They

climbed to a high bluff where it had been seen before.

"There he is!" said Charlie. "Let's get him before he knows we are here."

John took aim with his rifle.

"Now, John, don't you scare him off by firing and missing," said Charlie. "He's pretty far away."

John said nothing, but checked his aim carefully. All three men fired at once.

"I believe I got him, boys," said Charlie. They walked towards the wildcat. When they reached it, they found three bullet holes. Any one of them might have killed the great cat. Charlie and Cyrus looked at young John in a new way.

"You'll make a hunter at that, John," said Charlie.

John felt pleased with himself. "How about letting me try my hand at buffalo, Charlie?" he asked.

"I might do that some day," Charlie answered, "but your gun is pretty light for buffalo. It takes a good load of lead to bring one of them down."

They skinned the cat and then walked back to the bluff from which they had first sighted it. John stopped to look out over the plains. There was a valley below them, reaching far off to the west. The camp was off to the east. The others had turned to walk on towards the camp when John called to them.

"Look back there! Here comes a fine bunch of buffaloes—about twelve big bulls!"

Charlie looked back. Then he said, "There's your chance, John. Try your hand on them now. You've got the wind in your favor, if you cut over towards camp a little way."

Cyrus said, "It's too far. They'll be gone before he could get there."

But John had not waited. He was already on his way, and he did not hear Charlie's answer.

"It will give the boy something to do," said the old hunter. "Be the biggest surprise of the trip if he gets one of those buffaloes."

As John started down the slope, he checked his ammunition. He wished he were on horseback, but there was no time now to go back to camp to get a horse.

The trip down the hill was slow, for now and then it dropped straight down. John had to hold his rifle with one hand and vines with the other. At last he was down in the valley. He must reach the right place from which to shoot before the buffalo got there.

He set out at a run. Now and then he changed

his rifle from one hand to the other. He couldn't see the buffalo from there. He needed to reach the edge of the deeper "cut" through which they would be coming. If only he weren't too late!

His side ached from running when at last he reached the edge of the cut. Eagerly he looked for the buffaloes. There they were, coming along at a walk. The first one was about six hundred feet away.

"They'll pass me at about two hundred feet," John thought. "I believe I can get one from here if I wait until it is opposite me."

John waited. Then, at the right moment, his rifle cracked. The buffalo, taken by surprise, wheeled and tried to climb the slope across from John.

"I missed," thought the young man. Then he yelled aloud as one stumbled and fell down. "I got one! I got one!"

He hurried to reload and try for another.

Again he saw a buffalo fall. Even as it fell, he was reloading. He took aim at the leading buffalo. The animals were running now, trying to get away. The rifle cracked once more.

"Another one!" said John. The lead buffalo was stumbling. But John's cry came too soon. The animal did not fall, but turned and went back down into the cut.

John watched him for only a moment and then reloaded. There might be time to get another, for the animals seemed unsure of which way to run. He heard his next bullet hit something hard as it reached the buffalo. The buffalo he hit whirled around twice, and then ran toward the wounded buffalo in the cut.

"I must have hit him in the horn," John thought. He heard a great thud as the two big animals came together.

"I'll finish them later," said John as he took aim once more at a running animal. He took a long shot at the last buffalo still in sight, for they had taken flight back down the cut and had gone around a bend. He hoped his bullet reached the animal, but he could not be sure.

John ran forward a little way and then took aim at the animal who had been hit only on the horn. By this time, he had knocked down the wounded buffalo and was galloping away after the rest of the herd.

"Missed!" said John, and reloaded. He fired again, but the madly running animal went on and disappeared.

The young hunter ran towards the fallen animals. The first one he had shot was dead. The second was down and kicking. The third one, which had been knocked over by the other buffalo, seemed to be dying. He was lying on his back, with his great head rolling from side to side.

John walked towards the second buffalo. He dropped onto one knee, took careful aim, and fired into the buffalo's chest. The kicking stopped and the animal rolled over and was still.

"I wonder if I could still get that one that went up the cut," John said. He glanced at the beast whose head still rolled from side to side. He seemed to be slowing down. John was quite sure he had wounded a fourth buffalo, and wanted to follow it before it got too far away.

He ran up the ravine toward the bend, reloading his rifle as he ran. Then, suddenly, he heard a sound which stopped him in his tracks. He whirled around to face the roaring beast he had heard. The buffalo he had thought dying had got up. He stood now, pawing at the ground, his back arched and his tail straight up. Even as John watched, the great beast began to run towards him.

John almost turned to run from him. He stopped himself, knowing that he could not outrun the buffalo. The buffalo roared toward him as his fingers pushed the ammunition into place. It seemed he would never get that rifle raised to his shoulders, but he did. The buffalo charged onward.

John's finger curled around the trigger. "Crack!" and the buffalo was stopped. With one last roar, he fell. John's fingers shook as he reloaded and fired one more shot into the animal to make sure that he was dead. With a last look to make sure that no "dead" animal was about to chase him, John started again up the cut.

"I am sure there is a wounded buffalo up there," he said. He ran on. At first he could see nothing but grass and rocks when he rounded the bend. Then he saw the buffalo he knew would be his fourth. One shot finished him.

"Four down, with thirteen shots fired," John said as he counted the empty shells. They would be taken back to camp for reloading. "But Charlie will not believe me." He thought a moment and then walked towards his fourth buffalo. He took his knife from his belt and reached toward the great head of the dead animal.

"I'll take the tongues back. Then they will have to believe me," he said. He would not take the time to skin the animals. Tomorrow he could come back with the wagon. He finished the work of cutting out the tongues and hurried towards camp.

No one was there. John put on a kettle of water. He had the four tongues in it cooking when Cyrus and Charlie came in.

Charlie winked at Cyrus. "How is the great buffalo hunter?" he asked.

"Just fine, just fine," said John. "I'm cooking the tongues of the four I shot. Thought it would make a good dinner."

Charlie's mouth fell open. He stepped over to the kettle which hung over the fire. There was the proof that John had killed four buffaloes. Charlie held out his hand to the smiling young man.

"John," said Charlie, "you'll make a buffalo hunter yet."

Charlie was right. The next year, John was the hunter who hired skinners to work for him. He became one of the greatest of the buffalo hunters of the west.

BILL CODY AND BRIGHAM

The *wild west* was becoming a little less wild each year by the time Bill Cody was a grown man. There were still herds of buffalo in certain parts of the great plains, and there was still trouble with the Indians. But here and there were little towns. Ranchers were beginning to build up herds of cattle. The United States Army had soldiers stationed in forts trying to keep peace between whites and Indians.

Bill Cody had gone west with a wagon train when he was just a boy. He had been a pony express rider, a buffalo hunter and a soldier. He knew the west so well that he had served as a guide and a scout while he was in the army.

Then the shrill whistle of the "iron horse" began to be heard on the plains of Kansas where Bill was living. Bill needed a job, and he went to work grading the ground where the tracks were to be laid.

One day, Bill was working at scraping the ground but things were not going too well. His work horse had a bad leg and so he had hitched his fine riding horse to the scraper. The big horse, whose name was Brigham, did not take well to the work of a plow horse.

"Come on, Brigham," Bill said. "We have to get this job done."

One of the workmen watched Brigham a moment. He shook his head. "It is plain to see that Brigham knows he is above this kind of work. He'd much rather be carrying you into an Indian fight or on a hunt, Bill."

Just then someone called, "Buffaloes!"

Buffaloes had not been seen in that part of Kansas for several days, and the men were getting short of meat.

"Come on, Brigham," said Bill. "Let's do the kind of work we both like to do." As he spoke, Bill was removing the work harness from his big horse. In a moment, he had picked up his gun and was up on Brigham's bare back.

"Bring the wagon to pick up the meat!" he called as he rode away.

He had not gone far when he saw five soldiers riding out from near-by Fort Hays. They, too, seemed to be after the buffaloes. As he came close to them, Bill could see that one was a captain and the other four were lieutenants.

"Hello, my friend!" called the captain. "I see you

are after the same game we are."

Bill called back, "Yes, sir. I saw those buffaloes coming over the hill, and thought I'd go get them. We are short of meat."

The soldiers looked at Bill and his horse and turned to each other and smiled.

"They don't think much of my outfit," thought Bill. "And neither do I, for that matter. Brigham and I are both dressed more for work than for buffalo hunting."

As they all rode toward the buffalo, Bill could see that the captain was looking at his horse. Brigham did not look as if he could run fast. People were usually surprised when they saw what he could do. He looked more like a work horse than a saddle horse, especially when he was wearing the "blind" bridle of a work horse, and was without a saddle.

The captain called, "Do you expect to catch those buffaloes on that horse?"

Bill smiled over his shoulder. "I hope so, by pushing on the reins hard enough," he said.

"It takes a fast horse to outrun a buffalo," said the captain.

"Does it?" said Bill.

"Yes, but come along with us," said the captain.

"We are going to kill them more for sport than for the meat. We just want the tongues and a piece of tenderloin. You may have all the rest of the meat."

Bill kept a straight face, and even managed a "thank you." The six horses moved along slowly, as there was still time to head off the buffaloes. When the moment to speed up came, the captain signaled to the soldiers to follow him. The buffaloes were about a mile off on the prairie.

Bill did not follow but swung his horse off towards the creek which cut across the prairie. He said, "Those buffaloes are heading right for the creek for a good drink, Brigham. We'll go down to the creek and meet them there."

Bill's timing was good. He was right where he wanted to be when the buffaloes came near. They had begun to run, for the soldiers' horses were galloping after them. Bill pulled the "blind" bridle from Brigham's head. Now the horse was without reins for the rider to guide him.

"All right, Brigham," said Bill, and the horse was off. He was a trained hunter and knew just what to do. He started off at top speed. In a moment he was alongside the rear buffalo. Bill raised his gun — his favorite

which he called *Lucretia Borgia* — and fired.

"Got him in one shot," Bill muttered as the buffalo fell. The horse was gaining on the next buffalo. He was not ten feet away when Bill dropped him. On he went, from one buffalo to another, until all eleven were lying on the ground. Bill had fired but twelve shots.

He jumped to the ground. Brigham stood quietly, knowing the work was done. Just as Bill turned about, the officers rode up. Their surprise showed plainly on their faces.

Bill took off his hat and bowed low.

"Gentlemen," he said, "allow me to give you all the tongues and tenderloins you wish."

The captain had pushed back his hat and was scratching his head, puzzled. "Well, I never saw the like before. Who in thunder are you, anyhow?"

Bill held out his hand. "Cody is the name, sir," he said.

"Cody?" said one of the lieutenants. "Would that be Bill Cody who was a scout at Fort Harker?"

"That's right," said Bill.

The lieutenant turned and said, "Captain, this man has been hunting buffalo on these plains since he was in his teens. As for riding—he was good enough to be a pony express rider."

The captain smiled and shook hands again. "I'm mighty glad to know you, Bill." he said. "I had you sized up all wrong. You and your horse, too." He was looking at Brigham, who stood as quietly as if he had been tied in place.

"I can tell you now—Brigham is trained to hunt buffaloes," said Bill. "That is why I could get the animals, even though my horse had neither bridle nor reins. Brigham knew just what to do."

The wagon Bill had asked for came up then to carry back the meat. Bill took his knife and began the work of skinning and butchering as the officers watched. He set aside the tongues and tenderloins.

"We'll bring these to the fort for you," he said.

The captain held out his hand once more. "I'm proud to know you, Bill," he said. "You and that horse make a winning team."

It was not many months after this that Bill had a chance to prove how good a team he and Brigham made.

BUFFALO BILL WINS HIS NAME

Bill Cody had become known as a great buffalo hunter. But when people spoke of *Buffalo Bill* they did not always mean Bill Cody until one day he proved that he alone should have the name.

The railroad tracks were reaching farther and farther into the west. Great numbers of men worked at laying the tracks. These men lived in camps at the end of the line, and someone had to get meat for them.

In the heart of buffalo country, it was natural to feed them buffalo meat.

Bill Cody was asked to go to Hays City to talk to the men who were in charge of the twelve hundred railroad workers.

"Mr. Cody," they said, "we have heard that you are the best buffalo hunter in these parts. We would like to have you work for us as a hunter to keep our men supplied with meat. Can you do it?"

Bill thought a moment. He knew that the railroad line was to go through Indian country. To hunt there every day would be very dangerous. But he needed work, and he was not a man to turn away from danger.

"What is your best offer?" he asked.

"Five hundred dollars a month, if you can get twelve buffaloes a day for us," he was told.

Five hundred dollars a month! That was very good pay, Bill thought. His family needed many things. They would not like his doing such dangerous work, but that pay was too good to pass up.

"I'll do it," said Bill. He talked over the plans with the railroad men and started on the job right away. One man with a wagon was to follow him to pick up the meat.

He worked at the job for seventeen months. During that time he and Brigham became famous. He killed 4,280 buffaloes in that time with his old rifle, *Lucretia Borgia*. Several times his life was in great danger. One time Bill and his wagon man had to build a "fort" of buffalo hams to protect themselves in an Indian attack. At other times, the soldiers from a near-by fort came just in time to save the buffalo hunter's life.

Then it was that people began to call him *Buffalo Bill*. But there were other men named Bill who also were great buffalo hunters and were sometimes called

Buffalo Bill. One of these was Billy Comstock, chief of scouts at Fort Wallace, Kansas.

"We'll settle once and for all which one is Buffalo Bill," said the railroad men. "Bill Cody can beat Bill Comstock at buffalo hunting any time."

The soldiers were just as sure that Billy Comstock was a greater hunter than Bill Cody. A match would give them the answer. A day was set for the match and all over the west people talked about it.

"I'm for Buffalo Bill Cody," said some.

"What do you mean—Buffalo Bill Cody? That name belongs to Buffalo Bill Comstock," said others.

Just beyond the end of the railroad, there was still some very good buffalo country. The plans were made for the two hunters to meet there at eight o'clock in the morning. The one who had killed the most buffalo by four in the afternoon would receive a prize of five hundred dollars.

When the day came, a special train came from St. Louis so that people could see the shooting match. Bill Cody's wife and daughter came on that train, along with about one hundred other people. Soldiers from the near-by forts and people from the settlements came in wagons or on horseback. When the two men rode up to

the starting line on their fine horses, a large crowd had gathered.

"Are you going to win, Bill Cody?" called one of his friends.

Bill waved his hat where he sat on Brigham's back. His long brown hair hung down to his shoulders. "A mighty handsome man," people said of him.

"I certainly am going to win," he called back.

"What makes you so sure?" someone asked.

Bill patted Brigham's shoulder. "I have the best buffalo hunter under me, and *Lucretia Borgia* to help me. The three of us can't miss!"

Comstock's rifle was newer and faster loading than Bill's old 50 caliber rifle. But it was lighter, too. Bill was sure that the heavy load his *Lucretia* put into a buffalo in one shot would make up for the time it took to load.

"Ready, boys?" asked the starter. "One, two, three—fire!" The crack of a rifle marked the start of the big day. Cody and Comstock, followed by judges who were to count the buffalo that each man shot, galloped away from the starting line.

They had sighted a herd of buffaloes a few miles away. As fast as his horse could take him, each man rushed toward the herd. As they came near, the herd broke into two parts. Comstock swung to the left for his hunting, while Cody rode to the right.

"Circle them, Brigham," said Cody. Brigham swung around the herd, cutting very close to the leading buffalo.

"Crack!" went *Lucretia,* and the lead animal fell. The others swung away. But Brigham circled right on and kept them moving in a tight bunch. As fast as Bill could load his gun, Brigham had him in the right place to shoot another buffalo.

Comstock used a different way of getting at the animals. He started by shooting at the last buffalo of his herd, and then rode on to the next. This gave the buffaloes more time to scatter, and Comstock had to ride farther to catch up to the next animal.

"What's the score?" people cried as they reached the place where the first part of the hunt had taken place.

"Billy Comstock shot twenty-eight!"

Cheers rang out for Comstock.

"Hurrah for Buffalo Bill Comstock!"

But Bill Cody's followers were waiting for the judges to bring in his count.

"Thirty-eight buffaloes killed by Bill Cody!"

The cheering really broke loose then. But the match was not yet over. Once more the two Bills left the watchers and rode away to find another herd. This time, the herd they found was much smaller. As soon as it was safe, the crowd moved up to the new place.

"Comstock, fourteen. Cody, eighteen!" Once again, Bill Cody's backers went wild with cheering. The whole party had a picnic lunch there. The two hunters rested and joined the picnickers.

"Time to go again," said Comstock when they had eaten. "I have to catch up to you, Bill. Next herd, I'll take more than you will."

The ladies who had come to the hunting match looked up at the handsome man who sat on Brigham. "Don't let him catch up to you, Bill," they said.

"I won't, ladies. I promise you," said Bill. "But I think I will make it more interesting."

He got down from the big horse and took off his saddle. Next he removed the bridle. Then, with no reins to hold to, he mounted his old horse.

"He'll be killed!" cried the ladies.

But Bill just waved his hat and rode off, his long hair waving out behind him.

The next herd was found three miles away. It was very small—only twelve buffaloes in all. The wagons were quickly filled with people and headed out after the hunters. Those who had neither horse nor wagon to ride set out again on foot. Bill's bareback riding was something they had to see.

Some of the people caught up with the hunters while they were still working the herd. It looked for all the world as if Bill would surely fall off Brigham as the big horse swung into the herd. Bill was so sure of himself that he spent more time showing off for the crowd than working his herd.

"Look at Comstock go!" people cried. "He's really taking them!" Comstock had learned a little of Cody's way of keeping the herd together. He had already killed more than half the animals.

"Bill! Bill Cody! He'll get the whole herd!" cried some of the ladies. Bill swung around, waving his hat again. He popped it back onto his head just in time to aim *Lucretia* at one of the few remaining beasts. It was only the second one he had taken.

He swung around again, giving the people a show until only two buffaloes were left. Comstock was riding up to one of them. Bill pushed his knees into Brigham's sides and the good old horse turned towards the one remaining buffalo. The hunted animal swung around and headed straight towards the watching crowd.

"Look out! Everybody back!" people shouted.

Cody saw that this was no time for showing off. Brigham rushed after the buffalo, and Bill was alongside the great beast in a flash. His rifle cracked. The buffalo stumbled and fell.

Then the cheering rang out. The people knew how the match had gone without even waiting for the judges' count.

"For Comstock—fifty-one buffalo in all! For Cody—fifty-nine!"

Billy Comstock jumped down from his horse.

"I give up, Bill," he said. "I can't catch up with you—and you aren't even trying, now. You are the champion—Buffalo Bill!"

BUFFALO BILL
AND CONGRESS OF ROUGH

The wild west was gone not many years later. But Buffalo Bill kept it alive in spirit for the rest of his life. Long after the great buffalo herds were gone from the plains, he was putting on his *Wild West Show* in cities all over the United States, and even in Europe. He helped people remember how the hunters of America opened the westward trails for all the settlers who followed, first in wagon trains and then by rail.

124

ᵴ WILD WEST
ᵲIDERS OF THE WORLD.

WILLIAM CODY

ᴇ REAL ROUGH RIDERS OF THE WORLD, WHOSE DARING EXPLOITS
ᴠᴇ MADE THEIR VERY NAMES SYNONYMOUS WITH BRAVERY.

125